Sew Fun

FOR girls & dolls

SIMPLY STYLISH PROJECTS FOR COORDINATING CLOTHES & ACCESSORIES

ANA ARAUJO

Design Originals

an Imprint of Fox Chapel Publishing
www.d-originals.com

Introduction

Since the 1840s, many little girls have shared the joy of playing dress up and make believe with eighteen-inch fashion dolls. My mother owned a doll with a beautiful bisque face and curly hair. My own daughters, Juliet and Megan, spent hours of fanciful play with their American Girl® dolls. They had the luxury of their very own doll dressmaker—me! Now I'd like to share some of my easy-to-sew projects for today's little girls and dolls.

The projects you'll find here encourage children's creative imagination with fun and whimsical dress-up costumes and accessories.

Creating this book took a lot of creativity and support from many people:

A special thank you to Fibre-Craft Materials Corp. for providing the dolls Abby, Emma, Madison, Maria, and Olivia from their Springfield® Collection (*www.springfielddolls.com*) to model with our girls Loralie Balcunas, Emma Barney, Anya Dujmoric, Meredith Matsumoto, and Maddy McGowan (cover girl). Thank you to Olivia Bray and her mom, Laura, who showed me that today's girls still love to dress up their dolls! To Susan Hare, whose keen eye helps make sense of my creative world.

A very special thank you to the manufacturers that provided supplies to help create this book:

- Fibre-Craft Materials Corp. (Springfield Dolls)
- National Nonwovens (XoticFelt and wool blend felts)
- Beacon Adhesives, Inc. (Fabri-Tac fabric glue)
- Clover Needlecraft, Inc. (sewing tools)
- Phoenix Brands LLC (Rit Dye liquid dye)

I dedicate this book to Juliet Niczewicz and Megan Araujo for being the little girls whose hours of imaginative play have made them into the talented and creative women I always knew they could be.

Left: Author Ana Araujo with her daughter Megan.
PHOTO COURTESY OF SHANNON MONTEZ
Right: Ana's oldest daughter, Juliet, and grandson, Charlie.
PHOTO COURTESY OF CORINNE MCCOMBS

ISBN 978-1-57421-364-5

Contents

Materials & Tools

With some basic sewing supplies and tools, you'll be ready to create all of the projects in this book. Here's what I used to create these dress-up clothes and accessories. Substitute your choice of brands, tools, and materials as desired.

Sewing machine. Any sewing machine will work fine for the projects in this book. The stitches you will be using are the straight stitch and the zigzag stitch.

Hand sewing. You will occasionally need to use an embroidery needle and floss to embroider details or whipstitch the edges of fabric pieces together. I recommend using DMC embroidery floss in colors that match your fabrics.

Sewing tools. You'll want the following sewing tools on hand, ready to use: embroidery needles, patchwork pins, cutwork scissors, patchwork scissors, large measuring gauge, and ruler. (I recommend purchasing these tools from Clover Needlecraft, Inc.)

Specialty tools. There are some great specialty tools available to make your sewing and crafting easier. The following were used in this book: Pom-Pom Makers by Clover Needlecraft, Inc. (x-small, small, medium, and large) and a Crop-A-Dile hole punch and eyelet setter by We R Memory Keepers LLC (or a grommet tool).

Adhesives. Using an iron-on adhesive will make your projects that much easier to complete. I recommend Therm O Web's

Heat 'n Bond Lite iron-on adhesive. You will also want a fabric glue, like Fabri-Tac by Beacon Adhesives, Inc., and a hot glue gun.

Additional supplies. You will also need fabric dye (I recommend Rit Dye), buttons (I recommend those from Favorite Findings), grommets and/or eyelets, pipe cleaners, hairbands, yarn, ribbon, bandanas, and polyester fiberfill stuffing.

Fabrics & materials. You will see the use of gingham throughout the book, as well as flannel, cotton, cotton blends, fleece, tulle, and National Nonwovens XoticFelt and wool blend felts. Please feel free to substitute any of the fabrics and colors as desired.

A NOTE ABOUT SIZING

These projects can be enjoyed by girls of many different ages and sizes, so you may find you need to make adjustments to the patterns to meet the needs of your particular child. Adjust the length of headband and waistband patterns to fit the size of your child's head and waist. For other patterns, I recommend cutting out the paper pattern and comparing it to the size of your child. Make any necessary adjustments before cutting the items from fabric.

A NOTE ABOUT METRIC

Throughout this book, you'll notice that every measurement is accompanied by a metric equivalent. Inches and yards are rounded off to the nearest half or whole centimeter unless precision is necessary. Please be aware that while this book will show 1 yard = 100 centimeters, the actual conversion is 1 yard = 90 centimeters, a difference of about $3^{15}/_{16}$" (10cm). Using these conversions, you will always have a little bit of extra fabric if purchasing by the metric quantity.

IRON-ON ADHESIVE

Don't worry when you see some of the small pieces for these projects! It looks like a lot of sewing, but using iron-on adhesive will help make every project super easy! Whenever you see the words "Heat set," use the following process to make an iron-on appliqué piece. Note: These instructions refer to Heat 'n Bond Lite iron-on adhesive. Be sure to refer to the manufacturer's instructions if using another product.

1. Cut a piece of fabric and a piece of iron-on adhesive a little larger than the pattern piece.
2. Iron the adhesive to the fabric piece following the manufacturer's directions, leaving the paper backing in place.
3. Cut out the pattern piece and trace it in reverse on the paper side of the iron-on adhesive with a pencil.
4. Following the pattern tracing, cut out the fabric piece.
5. Peel off the paper backing and position the fabric piece on the main body of the project.
6. Place a damp paper towel over the cutout and the main body. Press firmly for about 10–20 seconds. That's it! Super easy and quick!

Scan this code with your smart phone for a tutorial video on making the Fairy Flowers (see page 5).

Flower Fairies

Maddy and Abby are lost in a flower patch. With their leaf wings,
tulle leaf and flower skirt, and pom-pom and felt flower wreaths,
these fairies are ready to help the flower patch bloom.

MATERIALS & SUPPLIES

* Felt in chartreuse, green, and dark green
* 1½ yd. (150cm) of tulle in each green, purple, and fuchsia
* Iron-on adhesive
* Girl's and doll's tank top in fuchsia
* Pipe cleaners
* Grommet tool
* Eyelets
* ¼" (5mm)- and ⅛" (3mm)-wide light green ribbon
* Sewing machine
* Thread to match
* Safety pins (optional)
* Pins
* Scissors
* Wire cutters
* Marker
* Ruler or tape measure
* Fabric glue

FAIRY FLOWER SUPPLIES

✳ Lightweight felt in lavender, purple, fuchsia, and yellow (I recommend a bamboo/rayon-blend felt as it is lightweight and shapes easily)

✳ Embroidery thread in matching colors

✳ Embroidery needle

✳ Sock or fine yarn in white, yellow, orange, purple, and green

✳ Extra-small, small, and medium pom-poms or pom-pom makers to make these sizes

Making Fairy Flowers

You will use these fairy flowers on the fairy skirt, top, and wreath projects that follow. You may make as few or as many flowers as you desire.

1 **Prepare the pieces.** From the felt, cut eight #1 flowers, ten #2 flowers, eighteen #3 flowers, and sixteen #4 flowers in the colors you desire.

2 **Mark the centers.** Using the pattern, mark the center circle on each flower. Cut a small hole in the very center of the each flower.

3 **Stitch the center.** Baste around the center circle of each flower using two pieces of embroidery thread. Start and end in the same place. Leave two tails of thread; you'll use these later to complete the gather.

4 **Make the pom-poms.** Following the manufacturer's instructions, make one pom-pom for each flower. Vary the sizes and the colors of pom-poms as desired. Note: Making pom-poms takes some time—it's a good project to do while watching a movie. If desired, you can purchase pom-poms and use fabric glue to attach them to your flowers. Once the pom-poms are attached, gather the flowers as described below and stitch a piece of yarn to the back of the flower to use as a tie.

5 **Shape the pom-poms.** Shake out each pom-pom and trim it into a ball. For a fluffy pom-pom, rub your fingers between the yarn's fibers.

6 **Attach the pom-poms.** Push the yarn tails from a pom-pom through the cut opening in the center of a felt flower. Repeat with the remaining pom-poms and flowers.

7 **Gather the flower.** Hold the pom-pom yarn tails to keep the pom-pom against the flower. Pull the basting thread tails to gather the flower around the pom-pom. Knot the basting threads and trim off any excess. DO NOT trim the pom-pom tails.

8 **Finish the flowers.** Adjust the flower petals as desired to create a perfect flower look.

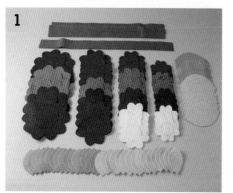

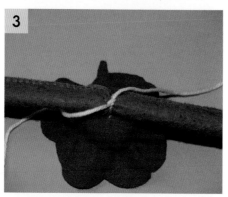

Flower Fairy Head Wreath

This head wreath can be made with as few or as many flowers as you desire, and in any color you like!

1 **Prepare the pieces.** From the felt, cut the desired number of flowers for each wreath, and a corresponding number of #1 and #2 leaves in green and chartreuse. From dark green felt, cut one large and one small wreath headband. Make the flowers following the instructions on page 5.

2 **Sew the bands.** Sew the two headband pieces for each wreath together along the short ends. Fold each headband piece in half lengthwise, and zigzag stitch along the long edge, leaving the ends open. Fold back ¼" (0.5cm) of each end of the pipe cleaners. Slip one pipe cleaner into the small headband casing and two pipe cleaners into the large headband casing.

3 **Attach the flowers.** Find the center of the headband. Place a drop of fabric glue on the back of a flower, and tie and double knot it to the center point of the headband. Repeat with the remaining flowers along the length of the headband, varying the size and color of the flowers.

4 **Attach the leaves.** Put a drop of fabric glue on one end of each leaf. Pinch the ends of the leaves and pin them in place to dry. When the glue has dried, remove the pins, and glue the leaves in between the flowers.

5 **Finish the wreath.** Stitch the ends of the wreath together, and tie on ribbons to hang down the back.

Flower Fairy Top & Wings

This adorable top is made using a child's tank top, meaning you can finish it in minutes!

1 **Cut the vine.** To make the vine, measure across the tank top from the shoulder to the opposite side. Cut a 1½" (4cm) piece of felt to this length. For the doll, cut a 1" x 6½" (2.5 x 16.5cm) piece of felt. Fold the vine pieces in half lengthwise and zigzag stitch along the long edge.

2 **Attach the flowers.** Following the instructions for the wreath (see page 6), attach the flowers and leaves to the vines.

3 **Sew the vines in place.** Hand stitch the vines to the tank tops.

4 **Prepare the wing pieces.** From the felt, cut four dark green and four chartreuse wings each for the doll and girl. Cut two dark green wing base pieces each for the doll and girl.

5 **Pin and stitch the wing leaves.** To make the wings, pair two leaves of the same color together and pin the edges. Repeat with the remaining leaves. Zigzag stitch around the edges of the leaf pairs, leaving an opening as shown on the pattern. Create the casing for the pipe cleaners by sewing ½" (1.5cm) in from the zigzag edge.

6 **Add the pipe cleaners.** Fold over ¼" (0.5cm) of the end of each pipe cleaner to blunt the end. Then, push a pipe cleaner through the opening at the bottom of each leaf and into the casing on each side.

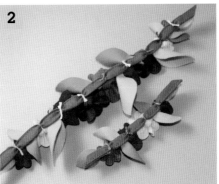

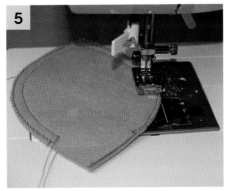

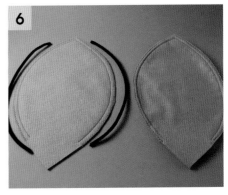

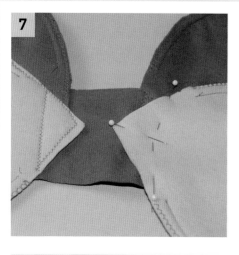

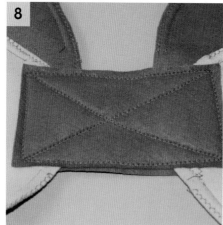

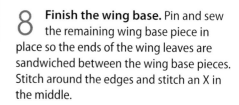

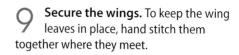

7 **Attach the wings to the wing base.** Pin the dark green wing leaves to the top of one of the wing base pieces. Sew them in place. Then, pin the chartreuse wing leaves so they overlap the dark green wing leaves and sew them to the wing base.

8 **Finish the wing base.** Pin and sew the remaining wing base piece in place so the ends of the wing leaves are sandwiched between the wing base pieces. Stitch around the edges and stitch an X in the middle.

9 **Secure the wings.** To keep the wing leaves in place, hand stitch them together where they meet.

10 **Attach the wings.** Safety pin or sew the wings to the back of the top.

Flower Fairy Skirt

The colorful tulle used to make this piece gives the skirt a dreamy, ethereal look—perfect for a little fairy!

1. **Prepare the skirt pieces.** Using the patterns, cut out all the felt skirt pieces. Cut the waistband from dark green, the waistband leaves from chartreuse, and the skirt leaves from green and chartreuse. When cutting the large waistband, place the pattern on a fold and adjust the size to fit the girl's waist. For the skirt leaves, cut a 7" x 32" (18 x 81cm) piece of felt in chartreuse and green. Heat set the chartreuse and green pieces together, creating a double-sided piece of felt. Trace the skirt leaf patterns on the felt; cut out six small leaves and six large leaves each for the large and small skirts.

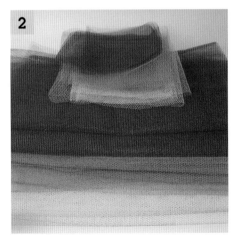

2. **Prepare the tulle.** Cut each piece of tulle into four smaller pieces. For the large skirt, cut 18" x 20" (46 x 51cm) pieces. For the small skirt, cut 6" x 8" (15 x 20cm) pieces. Stack two pieces of the same color and pin them along one of the long edges. Using a sewing machine, make a basting stitch ½" (1.5cm) from the pinned edge to gather the tulle. Repeat with the remaining pieces.

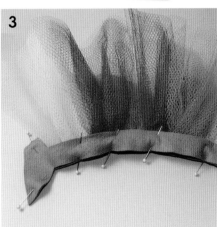

3. **Attach the tulle.** For each skirt, pin the six pairs of gathered tulle to one of the waistband pieces. Sew them in place using a zigzag stitch.

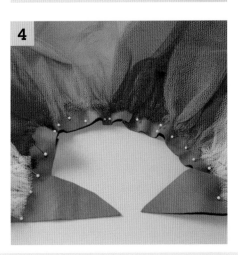

4. **Attach the remaining waistband piece.** Pin the remaining waistband piece over top of the tulle and zigzag stitch around the edges.

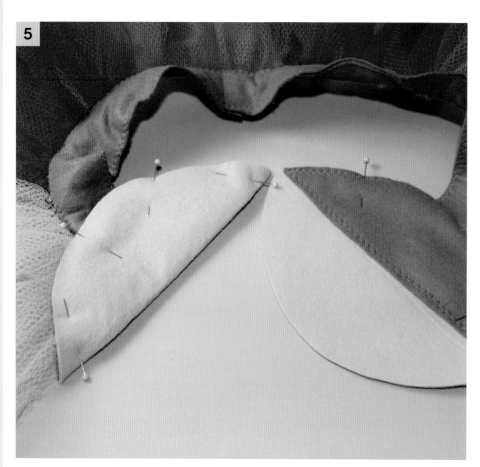

5 **Attach the end leaves.** Attach iron-on adhesive to the two waistband leaves, and remove the paper backing. Fold the waistband leaves around the half leaves at the ends of the waistband to cover them. Pin the leaves in place and heat set them.

6 **Finish the skirt.** Pin a small skirt leaf on top of each large skirt leaf. Using a grommet tool, add eyelets to the half leaves at the ends of the waistband as indicated by the pattern. Use eyelets to attach the stacked skirt leaves to the waistband. Tie flowers in place at the top of each leaf pair.

7 **Add the ribbon.** Weave the ribbon through the eyelets at the ends of the waistband to create the tie for the skirt.

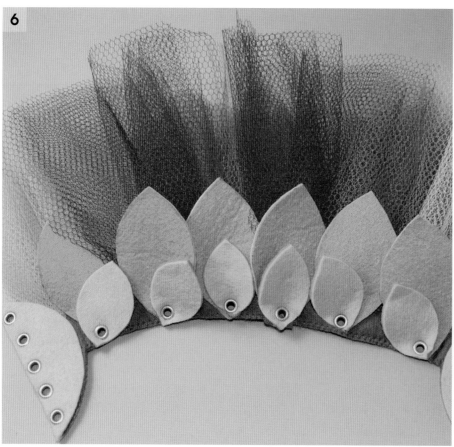

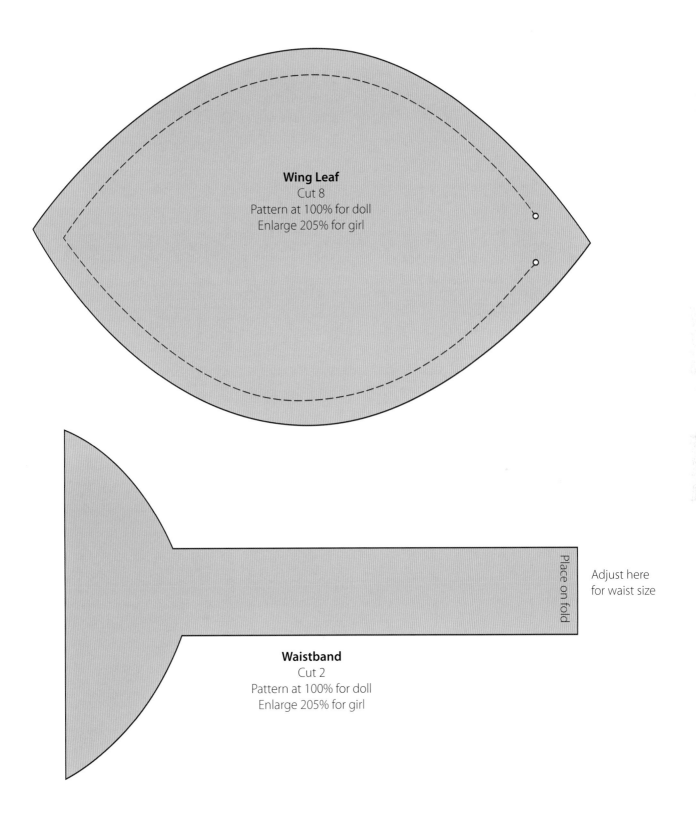

Wing Leaf
Cut 8
Pattern at 100% for doll
Enlarge 205% for girl

Place on fold

Adjust here
for waist size

Waistband
Cut 2
Pattern at 100% for doll
Enlarge 205% for girl

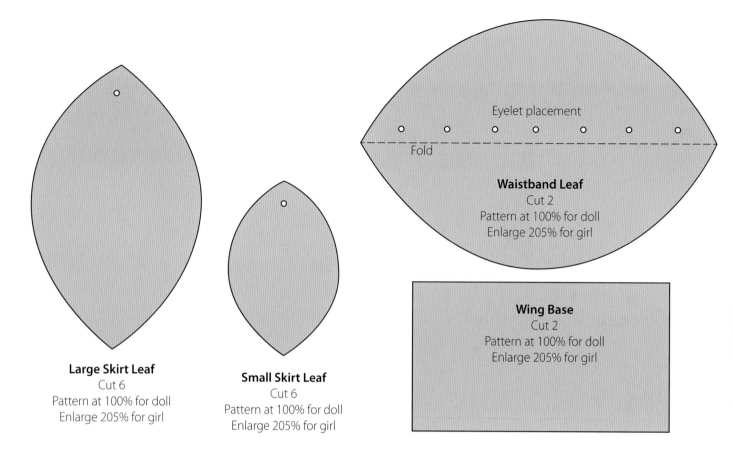

Large Skirt Leaf
Cut 6
Pattern at 100% for doll
Enlarge 205% for girl

Small Skirt Leaf
Cut 6
Pattern at 100% for doll
Enlarge 205% for girl

Eyelet placement

Fold

Waistband Leaf
Cut 2
Pattern at 100% for doll
Enlarge 205% for girl

Wing Base
Cut 2
Pattern at 100% for doll
Enlarge 205% for girl

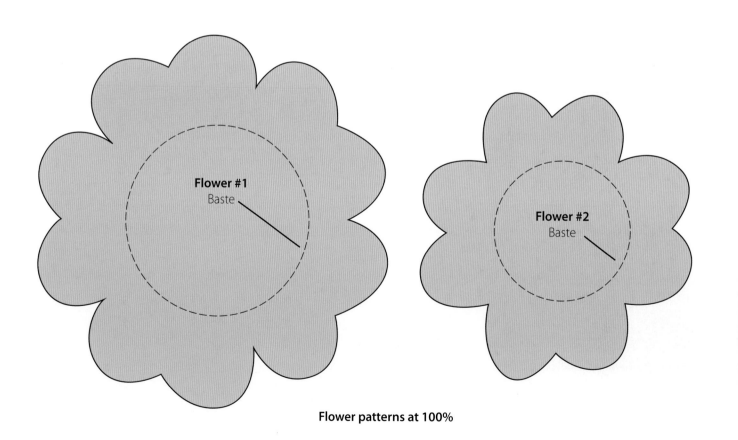

Flower #1
Baste

Flower #2
Baste

Flower patterns at 100%

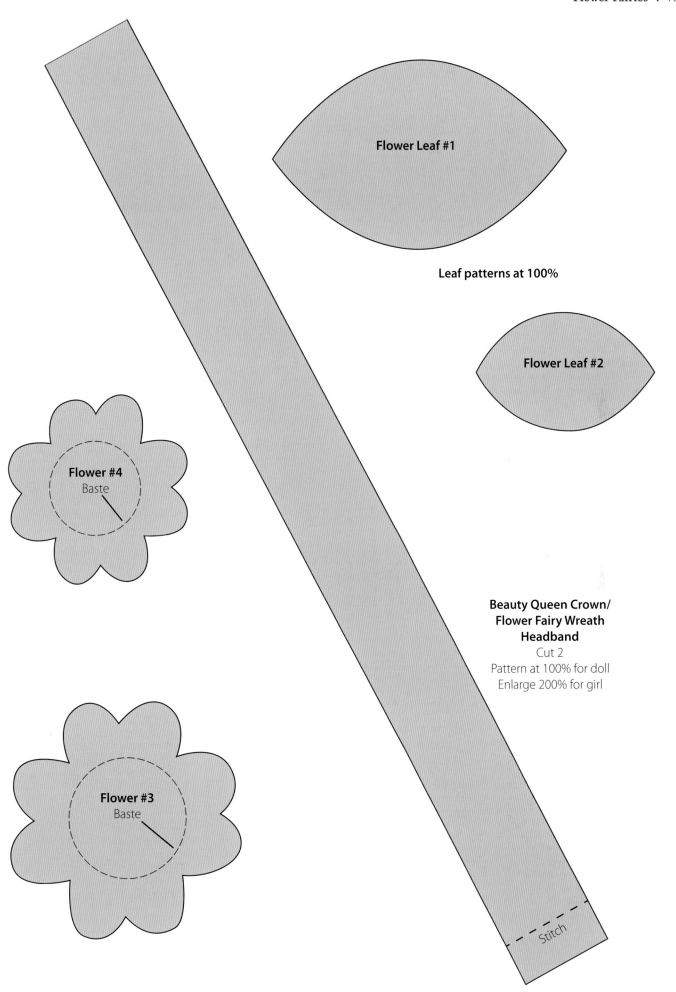

Flower Leaf #1

Leaf patterns at 100%

Flower Leaf #2

Flower #4
Baste

**Beauty Queen Crown/
Flower Fairy Wreath
Headband**
Cut 2
Pattern at 100% for doll
Enlarge 200% for girl

Flower #3
Baste

Stitch

Lovely Ladybug

Ladybugs are a garden favorite! Loralie and Emma, with their ladybug capes and antennae, are ready to fly away home.

MATERIALS & SUPPLIES

* ⅝ yd. (62.5cm) red flannel
* ⅝ yd. (62.5cm) black and white checkered gingham
* ⅛ yd. (12.5cm) black flannel
* Black wool felt
* Iron-on adhesive
* 2½ yd. (250cm) of 1½" (4cm)-wide black and white checkered gingham ribbon
* 1 yd. (100cm) of ⅞" (2cm)-wide black and white gingham ribbon
* ¾" (2cm)-wide and ⅜" (1cm)-wide black elastic
* Girl's and doll's tank top in red
* Embroidery thread
* Embroidery needle
* Ladybug buttons
* Pipe cleaners
* Safety pin
* Pins
* Scissors
* Marker
* Wire cutters
* Ruler or tape measure
* Iron
* Sewing machine
* Thread to match
* Black yarn
* Large, medium, and small pom-poms, or pom-pom makers to make these sizes
* Fabric glue (optional)

Ladybug Cape

The ladybug cape is cut to resemble wings, and has a lining that matches the checkered ruffle on the top.

1 **Prepare the pieces.** For both capes, place the ladybug cape pattern on a fold of the red flannel. Pin the pattern in place and cut it out. To use the fabric most efficiently, cut the large cape out first. Then, fold the remaining flannel in half and use it to cut out the small cape. Repeat with the checkered gingham. Open the cape pieces and press out the fold. Attach iron-on adhesive to the black flannel, and trace and cut the large, medium, and small spots for each cape from it.

2 **Sew the cape.** For each cape, pin the flannel piece to the gingham piece with right sides facing. Sew a ¼" (0.5cm) seam around the edges of the cape, leaving an opening for turning and two openings for the ribbon where shown on the pattern. Clip the curves and turn the cape right side out. Use a blind stitch to sew the turning opening closed. Hand sew a running stitch around the openings for the ribbon.

3 **Add the casing and spots.** To make the casing, follow the lines marked on the pattern to sew two rows of straight stitches along the top edge of the cape. Heat set the spots in a random pattern to the red flannel side of the cape. Zigzag stitch around the edges of the spots.

4 **Finish the cape.** For both capes, attach a safety pin to the end of the ribbon and thread it through the casing, gathering the cape fabric as you go. Make two large pom-poms for the large cape and two medium pom-poms for the small cape. Fold the ends of the ribbon over ¼" (0.5cm), and then fold them over ¼" (0.5cm) again. Sew a running base stitch at the bottom of the fold and use it to gather the fabric. Attach a pom-pom to each ribbon end.

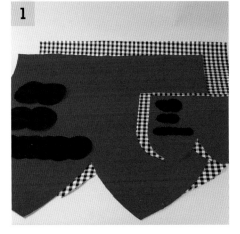

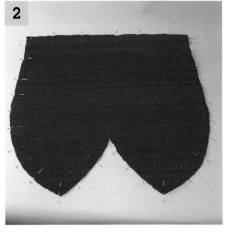

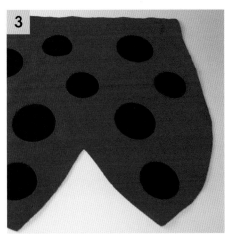

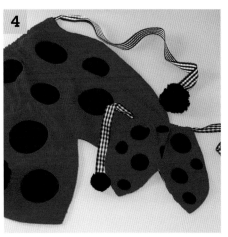

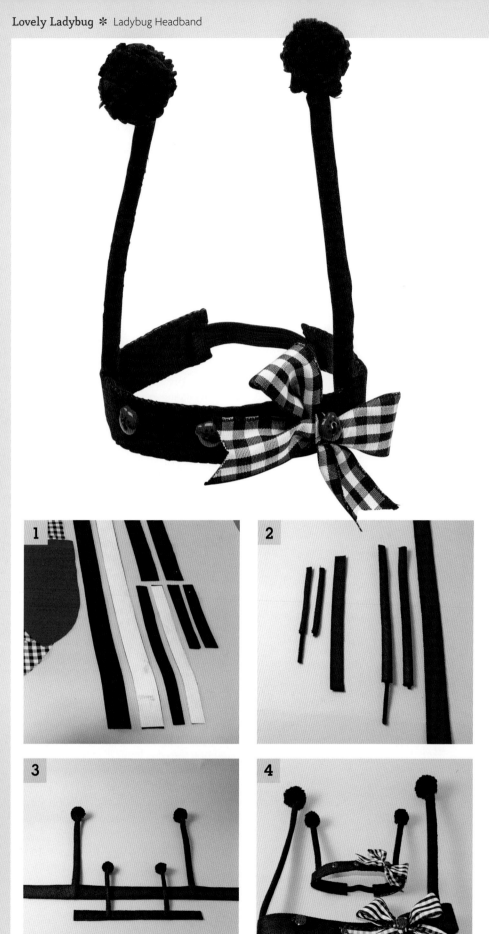

Ladybug Headband

The bow and button embellishments on this headband make it extra cute!

1 **Prepare the pieces.** For both the girl and the doll, cut the headband and antennae pieces from black felt. Heat set the two headband pieces together.

2 **Create the antennae.** Fold each antenna piece in half lengthwise and whip stitch along the long edge, leaving the ends open. For the large antennae, cut two pipe cleaners to 10½" long (27cm). For the small antennae, cut two pipe cleaners to 5½" (14cm) long. Fold back ¼" (0.5cm) of each end of the pipe cleaners. Slip one pipe cleaner into each antenna casing.

3 **Finish the antennae and attach the elastic.** Make two medium black pom-poms and tie one to each of the large antennae. Repeat with small pom-poms and the small antennae. If desired, use purchased pom-poms and attach them with glue. Measure the girl's and doll's head to determine the size of the elastic. Cut enough elastic so the headband fits snuggly without being too tight. Stitch the ends of the elastic to the ends of the headband. Stitch the antennae in place where indicated on the pattern.

4 **Finish the headband.** Tie a bow from each size of ribbon. Attach the bow to one side of the headband and sew a ladybug button in the center. Sew two additional ladybug buttons along the front of the headband.

Ladybug Top

To finish off the ladybug outfit, I embellished a red tank top for the girl and a red doll top for her doll.

1 **Heat set the dots.** Using the patterns, cut dots from black flannel. Heat set dots to each top and zigzag stitch around the edges.

2 **Measure and cut the ruffle.** Measure around the bottom of each tank top. For the girl, cut a piece of gingham that is 10" (25cm) wide and double the circumference of the tank top. For the doll, cut a piece 4" (10cm) wide and double the circumference of the doll top.

3 **Make and attach the ruffle.** Fold each ruffle piece in half lengthwise and make a running gathering stitch ¼" (0.5cm) from the fold. Gather the fabric of each ruffle until the length matches the circumference of the tops. Pin the ruffles to the bottom of each top and stitch them in place. I tore the edges of my fabric for an unfinished look. You can finish the edges by turning them under by ¼ (0.5cm) and zigzag stitching them in place.

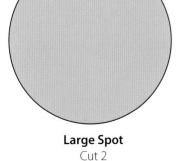

Large Spot
Cut 2
Pattern at 100% for doll
Enlarge 200% for girl

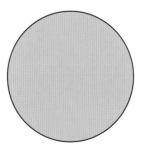

Medium Spot
Cut 2
Pattern at 100% for doll
Enlarge 200% for girl

Small Spot
Cut 6
Pattern at 100% for doll
Enlarge 200% for girl

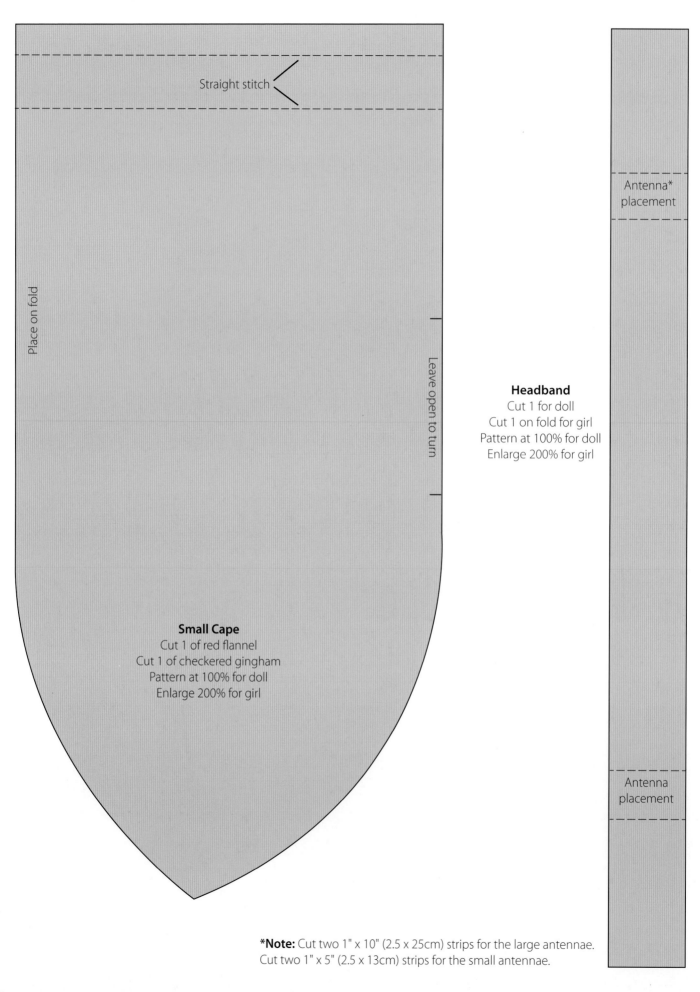

Straight stitch

Place on fold

Leave open to turn

Small Cape
Cut 1 of red flannel
Cut 1 of checkered gingham
Pattern at 100% for doll
Enlarge 200% for girl

Antenna*
placement

Headband
Cut 1 for doll
Cut 1 on fold for girl
Pattern at 100% for doll
Enlarge 200% for girl

Antenna
placement

*Note: Cut two 1" x 10" (2.5 x 25cm) strips for the large antennae.
Cut two 1" x 5" (2.5 x 13cm) strips for the small antennae.

A Day at the Beach

Maddy and Olivia are off to the beach in matching beach cover-ups. A single dyed bath towel has enough fabric to make both the girl and doll cover-up! The beach bucket purse is the perfect place for sunscreen and seashells.

MATERIALS & SUPPLIES

* 1 white 100-percent cotton bath towel
* Blue fabric dye
* ½ yd. (50cm) of each dark, medium, and light blue flannel
* Felt in orange and light green
* Iron-on adhesive
* Embroidery thread in royal blue and orange
* Embroidery needle
* Twenty-three ¼" (0.5cm) buttons in dark and light blue
* ¼" (0.5cm)-wide ribbon in two shades of blue and orange
* 1 blue beach bucket
* Cardboard
* Hook-and-loop tape
* Pins
* Scissors
* Marker
* Iron
* Seam ripper
* Ruler or tape measure
* Hot glue gun
* Hot glue
* Fabric glue
* Sewing machine
* Thread to match

Beach Cover-Up

This adorable cover-up doubles as a towel for drying off or sunbathing!

1 **Prepare the fabrics.** Preshrink the flannel and towel. Following the manufacturer's instructions, dye the towel blue.

2 **Cut the towel to size.** Cut the towel to approximately 23⅓" x 36½" (60 x 93cm). Adjust these measurements as necessary to fit the size of the girl. Cut the leftover towel piece to 7½" x 15½" (19 x 40cm) for the doll.

3 **Finish the edges.** Finish any cut edges of the towel pieces by folding them over ½" (1cm) and zigzag stitching them in place.

4 **Cut the waves and fish.** Cut the dark blue flannel into a 6" x 36" (15 x 91cm) strip and a 4" x 13" (10 x 33cm) strip. Repeat with the medium blue flannel. Cut the light blue flannel into a 3½" x 36" (9 x 91cm) strip and a 2" x 13" (5 x 33cm) strip. Attach iron-on adhesive to each of the flannel pieces. Then, trace and cut the waves from them using the patterns. Attach iron-on adhesive to the green and orange felt pieces. From the orange felt, cut nine small fish, eight big fish, and six small fins. From the light green felt, cut six small fish, nine small fins, and eight big fins.

5 **Attach the waves.** Heat set the waves to the towel. For the large towel, place the bottom of the top wave 10" from the edge of the towel. Place the bottom of the middle wave 5" from the edge of the towel, and align the bottom edges of the towel and bottom wave. For the small towel, place the top wave 3" from the edge, the middle wave 1" from the edge, and align the bottom wave with the edge. Zigzag stitch around the edges of all the waves.

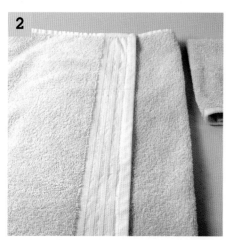

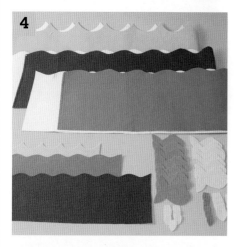

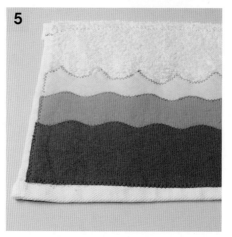

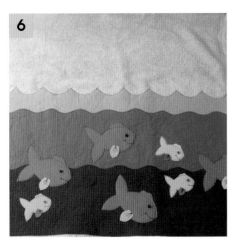

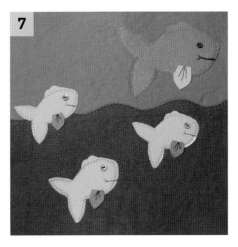

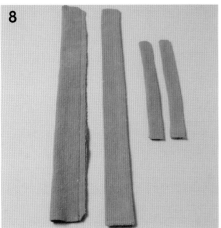

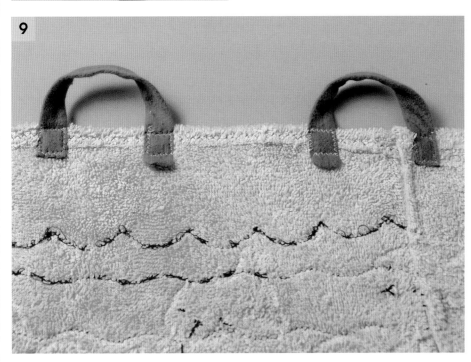

6 **Attach the fish.** Heat set five small orange fish to the small towel. Heat set five large orange fish and six small green fish to the large towel. Heat set green fins on the orange fish and orange fins on the green fish. Note: You will have leftover fish after this step to use for the bucket purse.

7 **Add the details.** Zigzag stitch around the edges of all the fish. Hand stitch three lines of varying sizes on the fins, embroider the mouths, and sew on the button eyes.

8 **Make the shoulder straps.** Using the pattern, cut out two straps for the girl. Cut two ¾" x 5½" (2 x 14cm) strips of fabric for the doll's straps. Adjust the size of the straps as necessary to fit the girl. Fold the strap pieces in half lengthwise and sew along the long edge, leaving the ends open. Turn the straps right side out.

9 **Attach the straps.** Using a box stitch, sew the shoulder straps to the back side of the cover-up. Adjust the placement as necessary to fit the doll and girl. Sew corresponding pieces of hook-and-loop tape to each end of the towel, placing one piece on the front and one piece on the back so they match up when the cover-up is closed. Adjust the placement as needed.

Beach Bucket Purse

This project takes the classic beach bucket and turns it into the perfect beach purse. The size makes it great for holding sunglasses, sunscreen, or a hat.

1 **Prepare the bucket.** Remove the handle from the bucket, and set it aside. Punch holes around the top edge of the bucket using a Crop-A-Dile hole punch or similar tool.

2 **Sew the lining.** Cut two 12" x 20" (31 x 51cm) pieces of light blue flannel. Pin the pieces together with right sides facing. Then, sew along the short edges to form a tube. Press the seams open. Form a casing by folding the top edge of the tube down ¼" (0.5cm), pressing it in place, and folding it down another ¼" (0.5cm). Sew the casing by pinning the folds in place and top stitching close to the bottom edge. On the bottom edge of the lining, sew two rows of basting stitches.

3 **Open the casing.** Using a seam ripper, carefully open the sewn side seams from the top of the casing to the bottom of the casing where it is stitched. This will allow you to thread ribbon through the casing for the purse closure.

4 **Gather the bottom of the lining.** Pull on the threads that form the basting stitches at the bottom of the lining to gather the fabric.

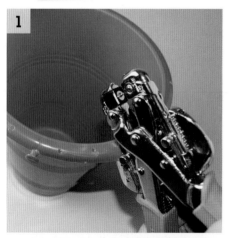

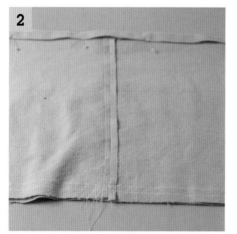

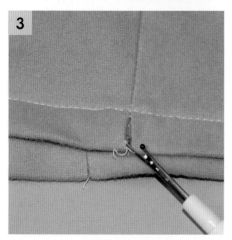

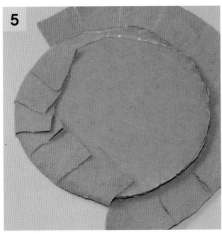

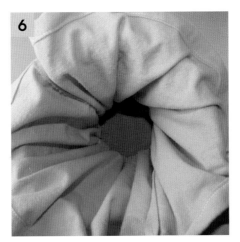

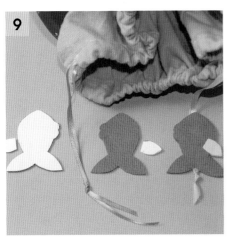

5 **Make the lining bottom.** Trace the bottom of the bucket onto a piece of cardboard. Cut a circle of medium blue flannel cut about 1" (2.5cm) larger on all sides than the cardboard circle and hot glue it to the cardboard. Clip the flannel edge and fold the cut strips up onto the cardboard; hot glue them in place. Make sure you pull the strips snuggly as you work around the circle.

6 **Attach the lining bottom.** Hot glue the cardboard base to the lining's gathered bottom. Position the cardboard so you see the covered blue side when you look into the lining. Then, cover the bottom of the lining with hot glue and quickly push it to the bottom of the bucket.

7 **Make the handle cover.** Measure the widest part of the handle and the length of the handle. Cut a piece of medium blue flannel twice as wide, plus a ¼" (0.5cm) seam allowance, and twice as long as the handle. Fold the flannel in half lengthwise and stitch along the long edge. Turn the cover right side out and slide it onto the handle, gathering the fabric as you go.

8 **Thread the ribbon.** Thread blue ribbon through the opening in one side of the lining. Loop it through the casing and bring it back out on the same side that you started. Knot the ribbon. Repeat with the remaining ribbon and the opening on the other side of the lining. Now, when you pull on the ribbons, they will close the top of the lining.

9 **Attach fish to the ribbons.** Attach a small orange fish to the end of each of the ribbon ties. Heat set the fish back to back, sandwiching the end of the ribbon between them. Heat set light green fins on the fish.

10 **Add the final details.** To finish the bucket purse, embroider the mouths and fins of the small fish and sew on button eyes. Heat set green fins on three large orange fish. Embroider the details and sew on the eyes. Using fabric glue, glue the three large fish around the bucket. Thread the orange ribbon through the holes you cut in the bucket's top edge.

Assembly Drawing
(For reference; not to scale.)

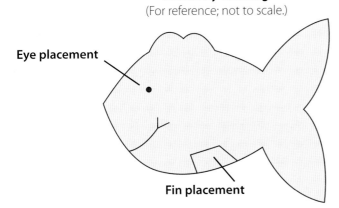

Eye placement

Fin placement

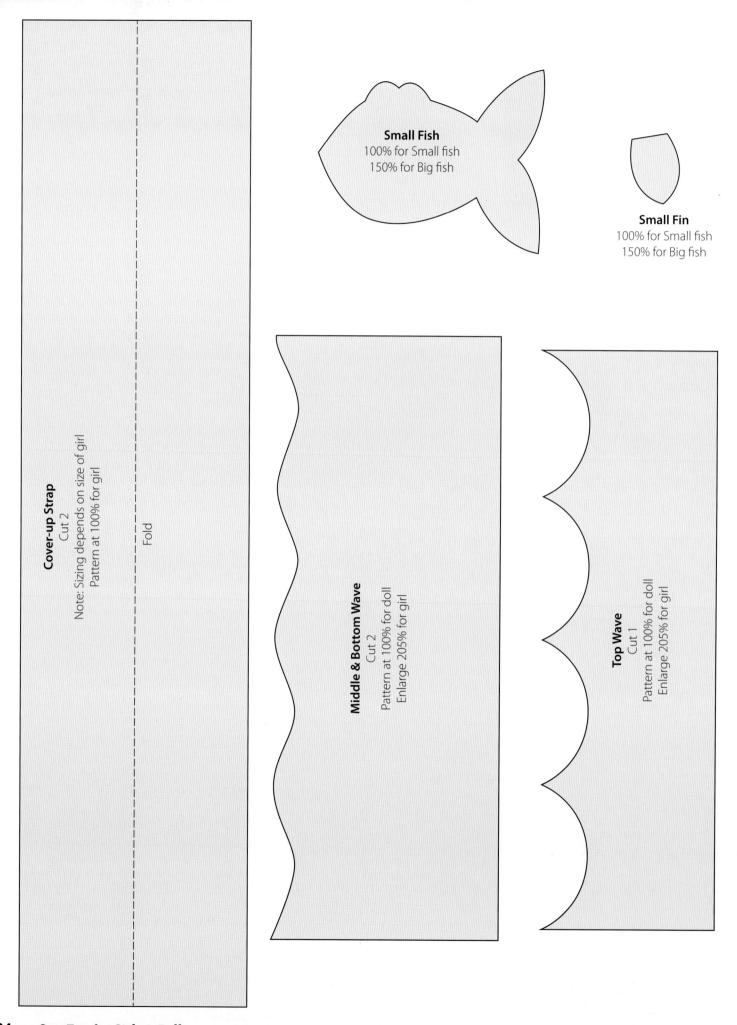

Small Fish
100% for Small fish
150% for Big fish

Small Fin
100% for Small fish
150% for Big fish

Cover-up Strap
Cut 2
Note: Sizing depends on size of girl
Pattern at 100% for girl

Fold

Middle & Bottom Wave
Cut 2
Pattern at 100% for doll
Enlarge 205% for girl

Top Wave
Cut 1
Pattern at 100% for doll
Enlarge 205% for girl

Beauty Queen

Every little girl dreams of being a beauty queen! For Meredith and Madison, their dream comes true with the Beauty Queen sash, glittery crown, and beautiful red felt rose bouquet. The Beauty Queen set will provide many hours of pageant play!

MATERIALS & SUPPLIES

* ✳ White faux polyester glitter satin
* ✳ Felt in blue, gray, red, and green
* ✳ Iron-on adhesive
* ✳ Holographic sequin strands
* ✳ Large and small faux rhinestone crystals
* ✳ Embroidery floss in gray and blue
* ✳ Embroidery needle
* ✳ 1 yd. (100cm) each of 1½" (4cm)-wide and ⅞" (2cm)-wide royal blue ribbon
* ✳ Green jumbo rickrack
* ✳ Pins
* ✳ Scissors
* ✳ Wire cutters
* ✳ Marker
* ✳ Ruler or tape measure
* ✳ Fabric glue
* ✳ Hairband
* ✳ 3 gray pipe cleaners
* ✳ 26 green pipe cleaners
* ✳ Sewing machine
* ✳ Thread in white, red, gray, green, and blue

Beauty Queen Sash

No beauty queen outfit would be complete without a white satin sash. Use faux glitter satin for this project to give it some extra sparkle.

1 **Prepare the sash designs.** Cut a 4½" x 12" (11 x 31cm) piece of blue felt and a 3" x 5" (8 x 13cm) piece of gray felt. Attach iron-on adhesive to both pieces. Trace the pattern for the lettering in reverse on the blue piece, and trace the pattern for the stars on the gray piece. Cut out the lettering and stars.

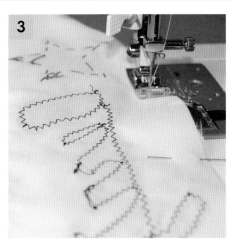

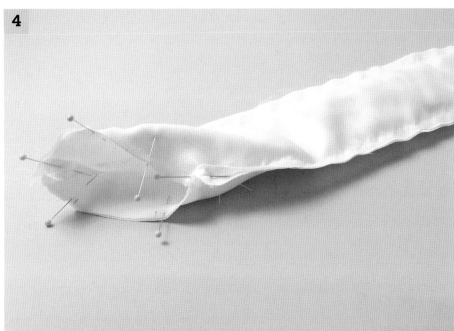

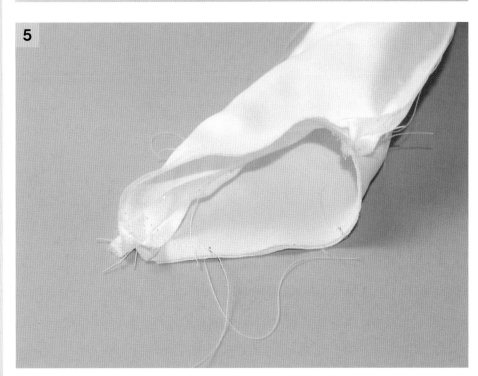

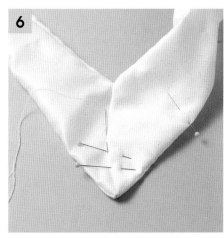

2 **Add the sash designs.** Fold the faux satin and place both sash patterns on the fold. Pin the pattern pieces in place and cut out the first side of the sash. Reverse the patterns and repeat for the second side. Heat set the lettering and stars to the front sash pieces. For the large sash, use the sewing machine to zigzag stitch over the lettering and edges of the star. For the small sash, whip stitch the edges by hand. If desired, hand stitch the sequin strands around the inner edges of the stars.

3 **Sew the sash.** Pin the front and back pieces of both sashes together with right sides facing. Sew ¼" (0.5cm) from the edge on each of the long sides, leaving the ends open. Turn the sashes right side out.

4 **Fold the sash.** This part can be a bit tricky, but trust me, it works! Begin folding down one end of the sash as if you were going to turn it inside out. Instead of turning it, though, continuing pulling the sash over itself until the ends meet. You will essentially have a tube with two layers of fabric. At the pointed end, pin the two layers of fabric together.

5 **Sew the end.** Stitch around the circular opening, sewing the two layers of fabric together. Leave an opening between the layers where indicated to turn the sash right side out.

6 **Finish the sash.** Clip the pointed corner of the sash and turn it right side out using the opening. Stitch the opening closed and press the seam.

Beauty Queen Crown

Coronate your beauty queen with this sparkling crown, complete with rhinestone crystals.

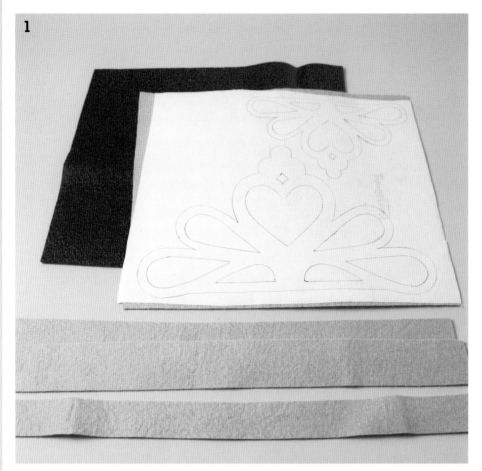

1 **Prepare the felt pieces.** Cut a piece of gray felt and blue felt to 8" x 8½" (20 x 22cm). Attach iron-on adhesive to the gray piece. Trace the crown patterns onto the gray felt and cut them out. Trace and cut the crown headband pieces (see page 13) from gray felt.

2 **Attach the gray and blue pieces.** Heat set the gray crown pieces to the blue felt piece. Cut around the edges of the gray pieces.

3 **Embroider as desired.** If desired, whip stitch around the edges of the gray part of the crown.

4 **Add embellishments.** Decorate the crowns as desired by using fabric glue to attach sequin strands and rhinestone crystals.

5 **Make the headbands and finish.** Sew the two headband pieces for each crown together along the short ends. Then, fold each headband piece in half lengthwise and zigzag stitch along the long edge, leaving the ends open. Fold back ¼" (0.5cm) of each end of three pipe cleaners. Slip one pipe cleaner into the headband casing for the small crown, and two into the casing for the large crown. Stitch or glue the headbands to the base of each crown and bend the headbands to the proper size.

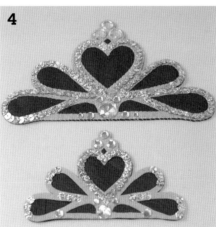

Beauty Queen Rose Bouquet

The flowers in this gorgeous bouquet will stay fresh forever! Change the felt used for the flower petals to make pink, white, or yellow roses.

1 **Prepare the pieces.** Using the patterns, cut twelve green rose stems, twelve green rose leaves, and twelve red rose petals from felt for each bouquet. Fold each stem piece in half lengthwise and zigzag stitch along the long edge, leaving the ends open. Fold back ¼" (0.5cm) of each end of twelve pipe cleaners and slip one pipe cleaner into each of the large stems. Repeat for the small stems, but use 6½" (17cm)-long pipe cleaners.

2 **Begin making the petals.** Using fabric glue, attach one end of a stem to the shortest end of a rose petal piece. Carefully roll up the rose petal, starting at the end with the stem and working toward the opposite end. Pin the petal piece in place. Hand stitch back and forth through the layers at the base of the rose petal and through the stem. Pull the thread tight as you go; this will shape the bottom of the rose.

3 **Finish the roses.** Cut twelve 4" (10cm)-long pieces of green jumbo rickrack for the large roses and twelve 3" (8cm)-long pieces for the small roses. Gather the rickrack using a running base stitch, and hand sew it to the base of the rose petals. Repeat for all the roses. Pinch the end of a leaf, and hand stitch it to the top of the stem, below the rickrack. Repeat for all the roses. If desired, fabric glue the leaves in place. Shape the tops of the petals as desired.

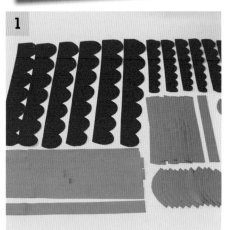

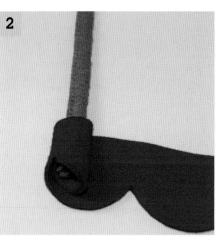

4 **Make the bouquet.** Gather the twelve large roses together and wrap a green pipe cleaner around them in the middle to hold the bouquet together. Tie a big bow over the pipe cleaner using the blue ribbon. Repeat for the small bouquet, but add a hairband over the pipe cleaner. Slip the hairband over the bouquet and tie it into a loop that can slide over the doll's hand. Tie a bow over the hairband and pipe cleaner.

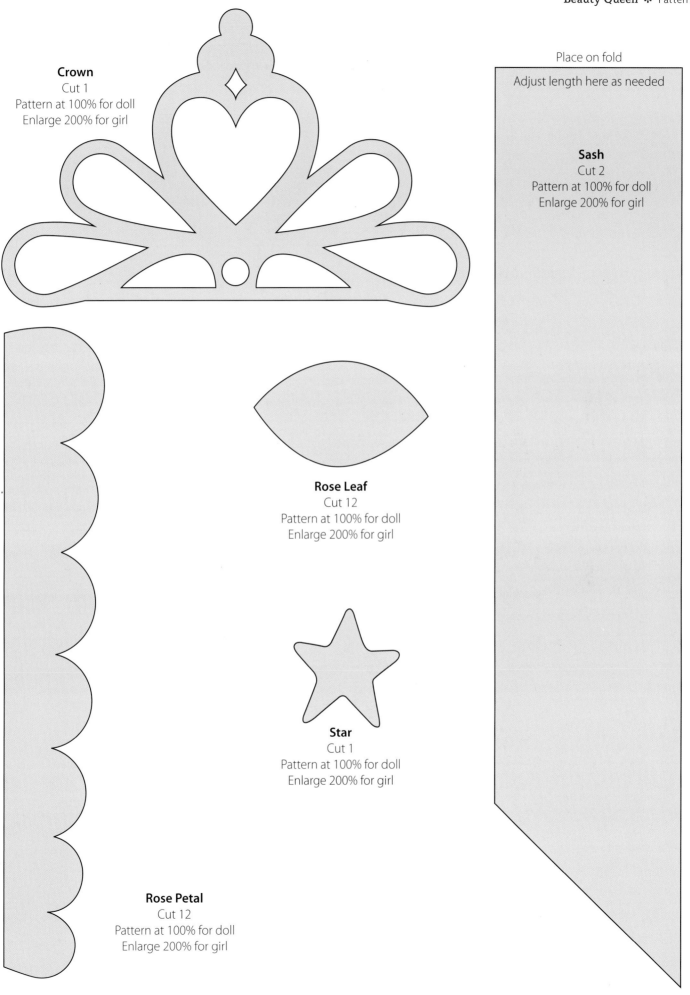

Crown
Cut 1
Pattern at 100% for doll
Enlarge 200% for girl

Place on fold

Adjust length here as needed

Sash
Cut 2
Pattern at 100% for doll
Enlarge 200% for girl

Rose Leaf
Cut 12
Pattern at 100% for doll
Enlarge 200% for girl

Star
Cut 1
Pattern at 100% for doll
Enlarge 200% for girl

Rose Petal
Cut 12
Pattern at 100% for doll
Enlarge 200% for girl

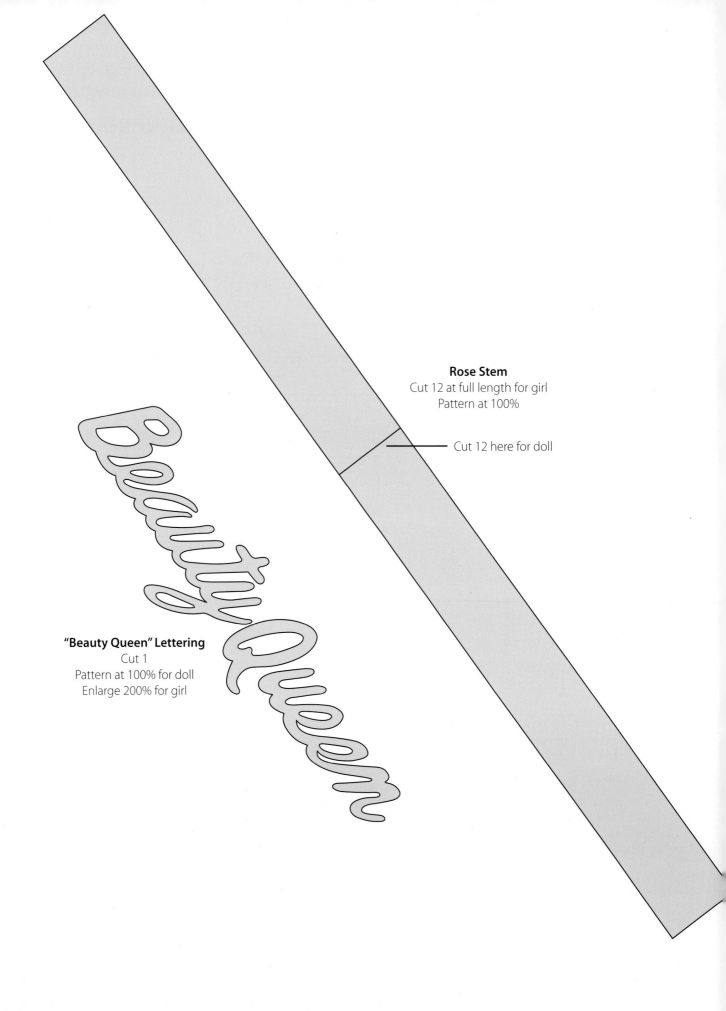

Rose Stem
Cut 12 at full length for girl
Pattern at 100%

Cut 12 here for doll

"Beauty Queen" Lettering
Cut 1
Pattern at 100% for doll
Enlarge 200% for girl

Cuddly Cat & Mouse

Anya and Maria are ready to go on a shopping trip decked out in a cat and mouse scarf made from knee-high stockings. A matching cat purse finishes off this ensemble.

MATERIALS & SUPPLIES

* 2 pairs of funky knee-high socks*
* Felt to match socks
* Felt in gray, pink, lavendar, and purple
* Iron-on adhesive
* Yarn to match
* Six ¼" (0.5cm) blue buttons
* Two ½" (10.5cm) blue buttons
* Polyester fiberfill stuffing
* Embroidery thread to match
* Embroidery needle
* Pins
* Scissors
* Marker
* Ruler or tape measure
* Sewing machine
* Thread to match

*You can use any color of knee-high socks. Just change the cat felt colors to match one of the colors in the socks. This way you can really personalize the scarf for the girl and her doll!

Cat & Mouse Scarf

You can make this project as funky or as refined as you'd like by changing the color of the socks you use to make the scarf. Go with neon colors for a playful look and solids or neutrals for something more classic.

For girl:

1 **Prepare the socks.** Cut off the toes from a pair of socks. Turn the sock inside out. Pinch the heel until there is no longer a bend in the sock. Pin and sew the heel in place as you would a dart, and then trim away the extra heel fabric. Repeat with the second sock.

2 **Sew the socks together.** Turn one sock right side out, and put it into the other sock so the right sides are facing. Pin the end of the tube with the unfinished edges together and stitch around the opening to join the socks.

3 **Turn right side out.** Turn the socks right side out. You will have a tube scarf!

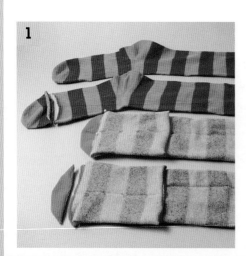

1

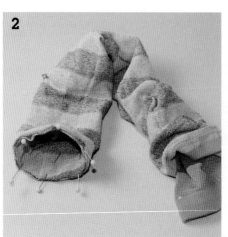

2

3

For doll:

1 **Trim the sock to size.** Measure 9" (23cm) down from the cuff of one sock and cut off this section.

2 **Form a rectangle.** Cut the sock open along both of the long edges so you are left with two rectangles of fabric. Pin the pieces together with right sides facing along one short unfinished edge. Sew the pieces together along this edge.

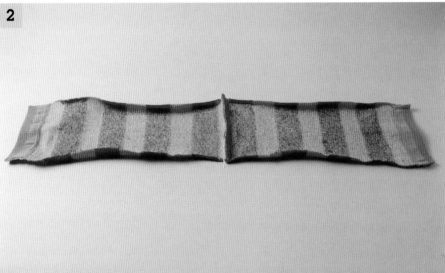

3 **Finish the scarf.** Fold the fabric in half lengthwise so the right sides are facing. Sew along the long edge and turn right side out so you have a tube scarf.

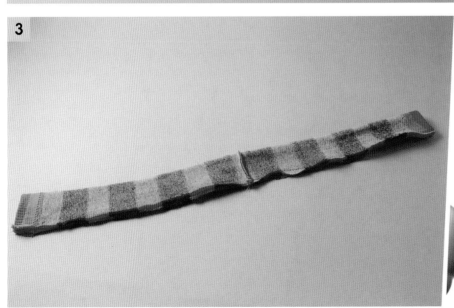

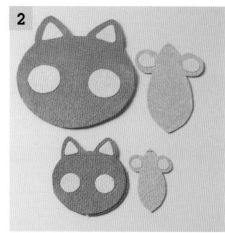

Adding the cat & mouse:

1 **Prepare the felt pieces.** For each scarf cut two cat heads in a color that matches the scarf, two pink inner cat ears, two pink cheeks, one gray mouse, and two pink inner mouse ears from felt. Attach iron-on adhesive to all of the pieces except the cat heads and mice.

2 **Heat set the necessary pieces.** Heat set the cheeks and ears in place. Mark the location of the noses and other face details. The noses can be embroidered or heat set using pieces of felt. Sew button eyes onto the cat faces. Use French knots to make the mouse eyes.

3 **Add the details and stitch in place.** Embroider the face details on the cat and mouse. Sandwich one end of the scarf between the two cat head pieces. Whip stitch around the edges of the cat head pieces, leaving an opening for stuffing. When you come to the top of the ears and head, only stitch through the felt and one scarf layer. This means you will stitch the front of the cat head to the front layer of the scarf and the back of the cat head to the back layer of the scarf. Stitch the mouse to the front layer of the scarf on the other end, leaving an opening for stuffing. Using yarn, braid a tail for the mouse and stitch it in place between the layers of the scarf. Stitch the scarf closed on the mouse end.

4 **Stuff, stitch, and finish.** Stuff the cat and mouse on each scarf and stitch the openings closed.

Cat Purse

This fuzzy feline purse is the perfect size for holding small essentials like lip balm, pencils, lunch money, and a phone.

1 **Prepare the pieces.** From lavender felt or another color that matches the socks, cut the purse patterns and cat heads for each purse. Cut a piece from the sock (using the cuff as the top edge) that matches the size of the rectangular purse bottom for each purse. Attach iron-on adhesive to small pieces of pink and purple felt. Trace and cut the inner ear and cheek patterns from the pink and the nose patterns from the purple.

2 **Attach the socks.** For each purse, line up the sock cuff with the top edge of the purse rectangle. Trim away any excess. If the sock piece does not have a cuff, create one by folding the top edge down ½" (1.5cm) and zigzag stitching it in place. Pin the sock pieces to the purse bottom with right sides facing. Stitch around the sides and bottom ¼" (0.5cm) from the edge, clip the curves, and turn the purse right side out.

3 **Add the face details.** Using the same method you did for the scarf, heat set the cheeks, inner ears, and noses to the cat faces. Embroider the mouth and whiskers, and sew on button eyes.

4 **Finish the purse.** For each purse, pin the cat face to the circular purse flap. Hand stitch around the edges using a whip stitch, or zigzag stitch around the edges using a sewing machine. Leave an opening for stuffing. Lightly stuff the purse flap and sew the opening closed. Braid the strap from yarn and stitch the ends to the sides of the purse.

1

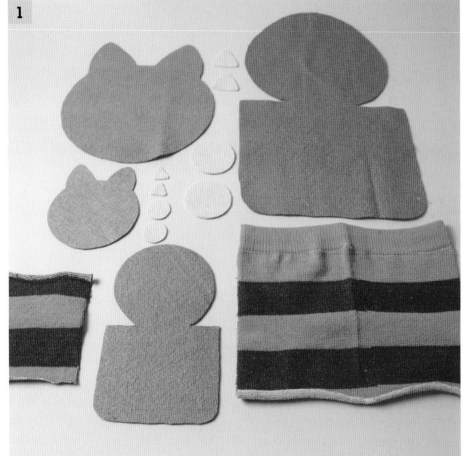

2

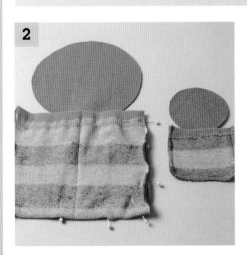

4

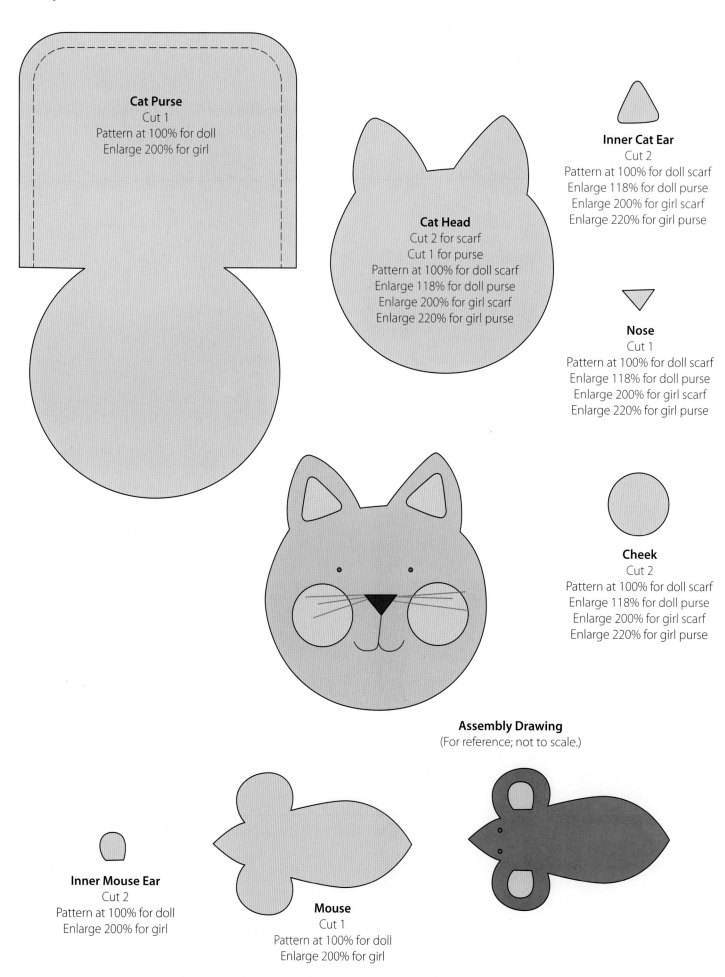

Cat Purse
Cut 1
Pattern at 100% for doll
Enlarge 200% for girl

Cat Head
Cut 2 for scarf
Cut 1 for purse
Pattern at 100% for doll scarf
Enlarge 118% for doll purse
Enlarge 200% for girl scarf
Enlarge 220% for girl purse

Inner Cat Ear
Cut 2
Pattern at 100% for doll scarf
Enlarge 118% for doll purse
Enlarge 200% for girl scarf
Enlarge 220% for girl purse

Nose
Cut 1
Pattern at 100% for doll scarf
Enlarge 118% for doll purse
Enlarge 200% for girl scarf
Enlarge 220% for girl purse

Cheek
Cut 2
Pattern at 100% for doll scarf
Enlarge 118% for doll purse
Enlarge 200% for girl scarf
Enlarge 220% for girl purse

Assembly Drawing
(For reference; not to scale.)

Inner Mouse Ear
Cut 2
Pattern at 100% for doll
Enlarge 200% for girl

Mouse
Cut 1
Pattern at 100% for doll
Enlarge 200% for girl

Classic Sewing Projects

Here are some super-easy sewing projects that any little girl is sure to love. Each
one can be customized with your little one's favorite color and is sure to be
enjoyed over and over.

Bandana Apron

Maddy and Olivia are cooking up something good in the kitchen with their matching aprons made from bandanas. This is a super-simple sewing project with a gathered waist and fold-up pockets.

MATERIALS & SUPPLIES

* ✳ 3 bandanas
* ✳ Thread to match
* ✳ ⅞" (2cm)- and 1½" (4cm)-wide gingham ribbon to match
* ✳ Pins
* ✳ Ruler or tape measure
* ✳ Marker
* ✳ Scissors
* ✳ Sewing machine

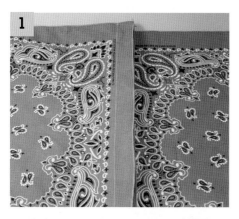

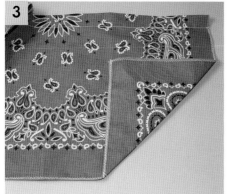

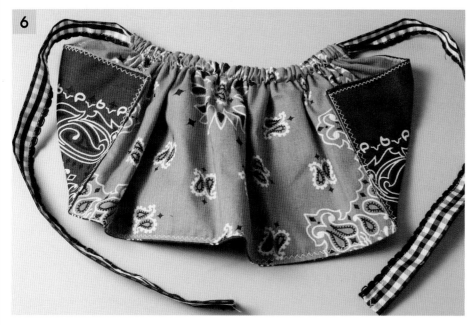

1 **Sew the bandanas.** With right sides facing, sew two bandanas together along one side. Use bandanas in two different colors if desired to give the pockets contrast.

2 **Sew the casing and edges.** Fold the bandana piece in half along the seam so the right sides are facing out. Make a casing by sewing 1" (2.5cm) down from the fold. Using a zigzag stitch, sew the outer edges of the bandana closed, starting below the casing on one side and sewing around to the other side.

3 **Make the pockets.** Measure 5" (13cm) in from the side of the bandana and 2½" (6cm) down from the edge of the casing. Make a mark at this point. Then, bring the bottom corner of the bandana up to meet this mark, forming a triangular pocket, and pin it in place. Sew straight down from this mark along the edge of the pocket to secure it. Repeat with the opposite side and corner.

4 **Add the ribbon.** Run the ribbon through the casing and gather the fabric until it measures 12" (31cm) long. Sew the ribbon in place at each end of the casing.

5 **Finish the ribbon.** Fold over and sew the ends of the ribbon to create a clean edge.

6 **Make the doll's apron.** To make the apron for the doll, repeat Steps 1–5 with two 5½" (14cm) square pieces cut from a bandana. Sew the casing ⅝" (2cm) from the fold. Mark the location for the pockets 3½" (9cm) in from the side and 1" (2.5cm) down from the edge of the casing.

Tooth Fairy Pillowcase with Pocket

Losing teeth is never fun, but collecting what the tooth fairy leaves behind is! This clever pillowcase has a tooth fairy pocket to exchange baby teeth for tooth fairy gifts. As an extra bonus, instructions are included to make a matching pillow for the doll.

MATERIALS & SUPPLIES*

* 1½ yd. (150cm) gingham flannel
* 1 yd. (100cm) star-pattern flannel
* Felt in white and pink
* Small piece of pink glitter tulle
* Iron-on adhesive
* Star buttons
* ¼" (0.5cm) blue buttons
* Pins
* Scissors
* Marker
* Ruler or tape measure
* Embroidery floss in white and pink
* Embroidery needle
* Sewing machine
* Thread to match
* Iron

FOR DOLL PILLOW:

* ⅜ yd. (37.5cm) muslin
* Polyester fiberfill stuffing

*Makes a standard-size pillowcase and a doll-size pillow and pillowcase

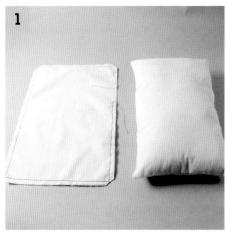

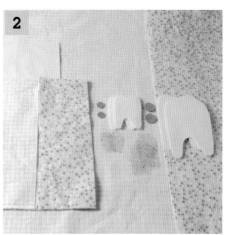

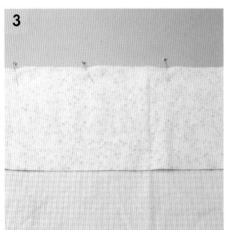

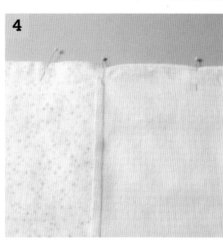

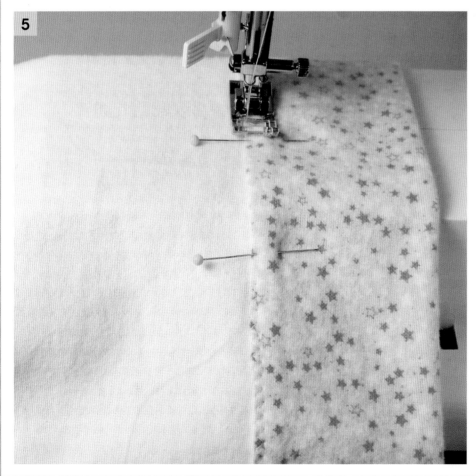

1 **Make the doll's pillow.** Cut two 8" x 11½" (20 x 29cm) pieces from the muslin. With right sides facing, pin the two pieces together and sew a ¼" (0.5cm) seam around the edges, leaving a small opening for stuffing. Clip the corners, turn the pillow right side out, and press. Stuff the pillow and stitch the opening closed. There you have it—a super easy doll pillow!

2 **Prepare the pieces.** Preshrink the flannel and press it immediately after drying. For the large pillowcase, cut a 21" x 26" (53 x 66cm) piece of gingham flannel and a 13" x 21" (33 x 53cm) piece of star flannel. For the small pillowcase, cut an 8½" x 9½" (22 x 24cm) piece of gingham flannel, and a 6" x 8½" (15 x 22cm) piece of star flannel. Using the patterns, cut the teeth from white felt, cut the cheeks from pink felt backed with iron-on adhesive, and cut the wings from the tulle.

3 **Attach the cuff.** For both pillowcases, place the cuff on top of the pillow base with right sides facing and line up the top edges. Pin and sew a ¼" (0.5cm) seam along the top edge. Open the fabric and press the seam toward the cuff. Hem the edge of the cuff by folding and pressing the edge down ¼" (0.5cm).

4 **Sew the pillowcase.** Fold the fabric in half lengthwise with right sides facing. Pin around the open sides of the fabric, leaving the cuff open. Sew a ¼" (0.5cm) seam along the two pinned sides.

5 **Sew the cuff in place.** Clip the corners of the pillowcase to give them a sharp point when you turn the fabric right side out. Fold the cuff back on itself, lining up the edge with the sewn seam. Pin it in place and zigzag stitch along the edge to hold it in place. Turn the pillowcase right side out and press.

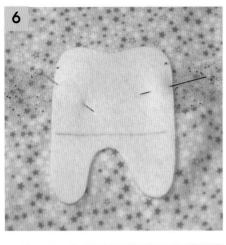

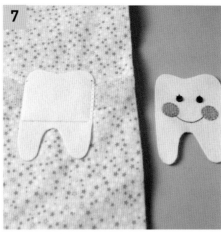

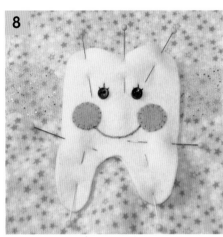

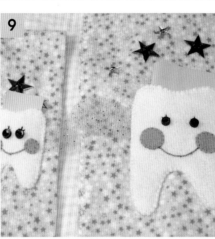

6 **Attach the first tooth piece.** Transfer the pattern markings to one of the tooth pieces and pin it in place on the cuff. Make sure you only pin through one layer of the cuff. Pin the wings in place on each side of the tooth.

7 **Sew the first tooth and prepare the second.** Using the pattern markings as a guide, sew the tooth pocket. Start at a top corner of the tooth and zigzag stitch down the side of the tooth and over the wing. When you come to the line, turn and sew along it using a straight stitch. When you reach the other side, turn and zigzag stitch up to the remaining top corner. Add the face details to the second tooth piece by heat setting the cheeks, embroidering the mouth, and sewing on button eyes.

8 **Sew the second tooth.** Pin the embroidered tooth on top of the first tooth. To keep the pocket open, pin the tops of the two teeth to each other and not to the cuff fabric. Pin the sides and bottom of the upper tooth to the cuff. Whip stitch the tops of the two teeth together. Continue whip stitching around the teeth, catching the cuff fabric as you sew around the sides and bottom.

9 **Finish the pillowcase.** Sew star buttons onto the cuff as desired. Put pillows into the pillowcases. When your girl loses a tooth, have her put it in the tooth pocket with a note to the tooth fairy. Use a grain of rice for the doll's tooth.

**Patterns at 100% for doll
Enlarge 200% for girl**

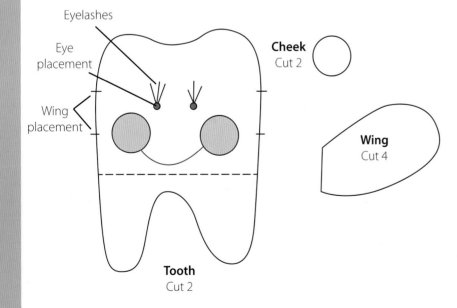

Eyelashes

Eye placement

Wing placement

Cheek
Cut 2

Wing
Cut 4

Tooth
Cut 2

Slumber Party Sleeping Bag

When it's time for a sleepover or a nap, these personalized matching sleeping bags with built-in pillows will keep your girl and her doll warm and cozy. They are made from fleece and flannel with cute-as-a button closures. For an added touch, you can personalize the sleeping bags with alphabet patterns.

MATERIALS & SUPPLIES

* ✳ 6 yd. (600cm) fleece
* ✳ 6 yd. (600cm) flannel
* ✳ Iron-on adhesive
* ✳ Hairbands
* ✳ Large buttons
* ✳ Polyester fiberfill stuffing
* ✳ Scissors
* ✳ Pins
* ✳ Marker
* ✳ Ruler or tape measure
* ✳ Sewing machine
* ✳ Matching thread

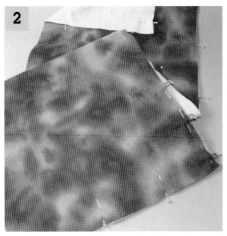

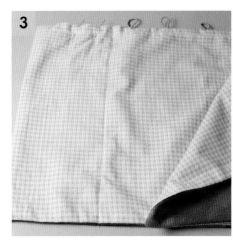

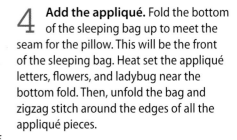

1 **Prepare the pieces.** For the large sleeping bag, cut a flannel and fleece piece to 30" x 124" (76 x 315cm). Note: for a taller girl, you might need some extra fabric. This project is designed for a 40" (102cm)-tall girl. For the small sleeping bag, cut a flannel and fleece piece to 13½" x 42" (34 x 107cm). If adding appliqué, attach iron-on adhesive to the back of the desired pieces of flannel. Trace the desired letters in reverse and cut them out. If desired, trace and cut out flowers or ladybugs.

2 **Sew the sleeping bag.** Pin the fleece and flannel pieces together with right sides facing. Pin three hairbands in the seam of one of the long edges, near the top. This will form the upper right side of the finished sleeping bag. For the large sleeping bag, pin the hairbands 1" (2.5cm) from the edge, with 6" (15cm) between each one. For the small sleeping bag, pin them ½" (1.5cm) from the edge, with 3" (8cm) between each one. Sew a ½" (1.5cm) seam around the edges, leaving an opening along the top right side. You will use this opening to turn the bag right side out and form the pillow.

3 **Sew the pillow.** Clip the corners, turn the sleeping bag right side out using the opening, and press. For the large sleeping bag, measure 13½" (34cm) down from the top and sew straight across the bag at this point to form the pillow area. Repeat with the small sleeping bag, measuring 5" (13cm) down from the top.

4 **Add the appliqué.** Fold the bottom of the sleeping bag up to meet the seam for the pillow. This will be the front of the sleeping bag. Heat set the appliqué letters, flowers, and ladybug near the bottom fold. Then, unfold the bag and zigzag stitch around the edges of all the appliqué pieces.

5 **Finish the sleeping bag.** Fold the bottom of the bag up to meet the pillow seam. Pin and zigzag stitch around the edges, sewing through all the layers of fabric. For the small sleeping bag, stop stitching 1" (2.5cm) below the bottom hairband. For the large sleeping bag, stop stitching 6" (15cm) from the bottom hairband. Stuff the pillow and hand stitch the opening closed. Stitch buttons in place on top of the sleeping bag, aligning them with the hairbands to be used as closures. Sew buttons onto the appliqué pieces as desired.

Large Flower
Resize as desired

Monogram Letter patterns
Resize as desired

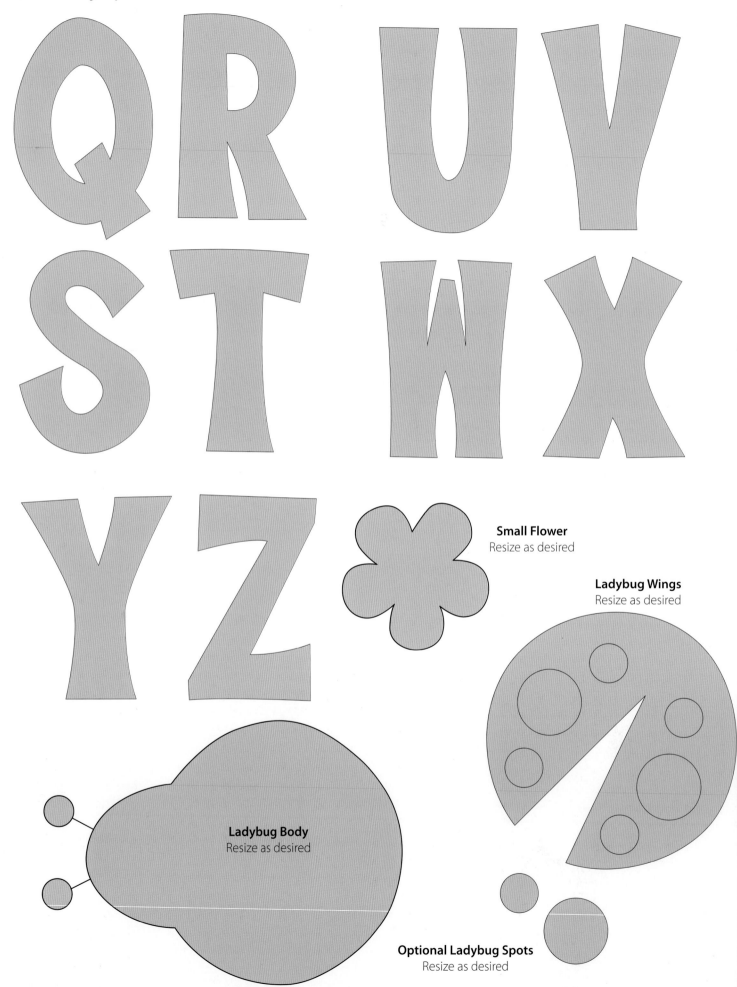

Small Flower
Resize as desired

Ladybug Wings
Resize as desired

Ladybug Body
Resize as desired

Optional Ladybug Spots
Resize as desired